Jesus in the Olive

A factual and scriptural look at the olive and it's comparison to the life and death of Jesus Christ.

Christopher B. Saylor

Heart to Heart *Publishing, Inc.*

Heart to Heart Publishing, Inc.
528 Mud Creek Road • Morgantown, KY 42261
(270) 526-5589
www.hearttoheartpublishinginc.com

Copyright © 2014
Publishing Rights: Heart to Heart Publishing, Inc.
Publishing Date 2014
Library of Congress Control No. 2014934810
ISBN 978-1-937008-31-4

Author: Christopher B. Saylor
Senior editor: L.J. Gill
Editor: Patricia Craig
Designer: April Yingling-Jernigan

Printed in Korea

First Edition
10 9 8 7 6 5 4 3 2

Table of Contents

Foreword 5

Facts of the Olive Tree 9

Harvesting Olives 13

Making Olive Oil 15

Olive in Easton's Bible Dictionary 19

Olive in Fausset's Bible Dictionary 21

Olive in Smith's Bible Dictionary 23

Olive Oil and Olives in Bible Times 25

Traveling with Food 29

Lessons from the Olive Tree in the Book of Psalms 31

Grafting: A Look at our Root 35

The Mount of Olives 39

The Symbolisms of the Tree, the Olive and the Oil 43

Sources 65

Questions for Discussion 67

Foreword

Ever since the third day of Creation, trees, in all their beauty, have graced the face of the Earth. These trees have been a valuable resource to mankind. They provide us with oxygen to breathe, building supplies for our homes, furniture, pencils, paper, food, beautiful colored leaves for our viewing, etc., not to mention shade on the hot summer days and warmth on the cold wintry nights. Of the thousands of species of trees, there are several that portray great characteristics, such as the mighty oak, the towering redwood, the whispering pine, the weeping willow and the list goes on and on; but, there is one that is worthy of notice, that being the olive tree. Most of us are not too familiar with olive trees because they do not grow near where we live. Just by looking at them, you can sense that they have characteristics that set them apart from all other tress. The olive trees, 'Olea europaea', are the oldest fruit trees and certainly are one of the most important trees in history. The writers of scripture have used the characteristics of the olive tree to tell us more about God, Israel and our relationship with them. In the Mediterranean region, it was, and is, the most important of all the trees because it is a source of wealth, food, light, and healing. The ten largest olive-producing countries are located in this region and produce 95% of the world's olives. The dependable fruit production and olive oil production means that the olive trees must exist in a peaceful environment, which is probably why the olive tree, or the branch of the tree, has historically been a symbol of peace and goodwill. It is only fitting that it is the first tree to be named "king" of the trees (Judges 9:8-9).

So, how and where does Jesus fit in with this? Let me explain: In the summer of 2013, after a church service, a fellow brother in the Lord asked me if I had ever looked up the word "Gethsemane." And, my reply to him was, "No, I don't think I ever have." He said he had heard a preacher on the radio say that "Gethsemane" meant "oil press." I found myself quite intrigued by this; so, I went home that night and looked it up, and guess what? I found the definition to be true. After finding this out, there was something inside of me, prompting me to look further into the matter, which I did. I researched some other information about this for my own personal knowledge, but the "prompting" kept driving me further into it. As I gathered some of this information, I thought that this could be a really good Sunday school lesson. Then I realized that it goes beyond a simple lesson to be taught. My studying had overtaken my everyday thoughts. I could not get it out of my mind. So, I gave myself over to the driving force that was pushing me and continued to read and search for more information. Every time I read something, it seemed as if I were reading about Jesus. He was in all that I read. I carried a list with me every day and when I would read something else that I saw Jesus in, I wrote it down. You now have most of the information that I have read and the notes that I have made in your hand. Since I saw Jesus in the olive during my study, I decided to entitle it the same, Jesus in the Olive. I thank you for taking time to read the book and may the Lord bless you, as he has me, with its teachings.

Although several months of research have been given to the writing of this manuscript, the result is not to be considered an exhaustive treatise on the subject.

- First and foremost, I give special thanks to the "prompting" and "driving" force behind this book, the Lord Jesus Christ. For without Him, this would not have been possible.

- I would like to give special thanks to my wife and son for their patience and understanding during my studying and writing.

- I would also like to thank the publisher of this book, a couple of fellow co-workers and a couple of fellow church members for taking the time to proofread this material and for sharing their thoughts about it with me.

Author's note: Concerning the picture on the front of the book: The stock of the tree is a silhouette of Jesus on the cross. If you look closely, above the top of the cross, in the branches, you will see the name "JESUS" in them.

WARNING:

After reading this book, you may never look at an olive or olive oil the same.

Facts of the Olive Tree

(001) Olive tree in Assisi, Italy

For centuries, the olive tree has been growing in lands bordering the Mediterranean Sea, but its growth in Israel has been quite abundant. Moses told Israel that Canaan was "a land of oil olive" (Deuteronomy 8:8). He also told them that they would acquire olive trees which they had not planted (Deuteronomy 6:11). From that day to the present day, the olive tree and the olive have played an important part in the history of the land. [1]

For thousands of years, even now, olives have been a staple food even of the poor. Olive oil has been used for cooking, in lamps for light, for anointing in religious ceremonies, etc. The trees were always, and still are, plentiful around the countryside and known for their tenacious ability. Even with minimum water, they can still thrive in great heat and are considered indestructible. Some grow from root systems that are over two thousand years old. Noah knew the waters had receded when the dove came back with an olive leaf in its mouth. The olive tree, regardless of whatever else had been destroyed by the water of the flood, had survived. One of the universal emblems of peace has been the olive branch. The olive branch was used on many of the Roman coins of the day. Following is a picture of a Roman gold coin dated 36A.D. Notice the olive leaves on the head and the olive branch in the hand.

(002) Gold Roman coin dated 36 A.D.

The olive tree takes between three to five years before it produces any fruit. It is between twelve and fourteen years of age before the olive crop matures and thirty to seventy years of age before the crop reaches its peak performance.

After the olive tree reaches its maturity, its fruitfulness lasts for many years. Its longevity is one of the remarkable characteristics of the tree. It lives and bears fruit for centuries. The olive tree, with its dull grayish color of foliage, does not seem to be a particularly beautiful tree, but it has many charms. Writers of Scripture often speak of the beauty and attractiveness of the olive. Concerning Israel, the prophet Jeremiah said: "the Lord called thy name, A green olive tree, fair, and of goodly fruit..." (Jeremiah 11:16). The prophet Hosea said, "...His beauty shall be as the olive tree..." (Hosea 14:6). And, David asserted concerning himself: "...I am like a green olive tree in the house of God..." (Psalm 52:8). Olive trees have a remarkable number of blossoms, many of which fall without ever maturing into fruit. [1]

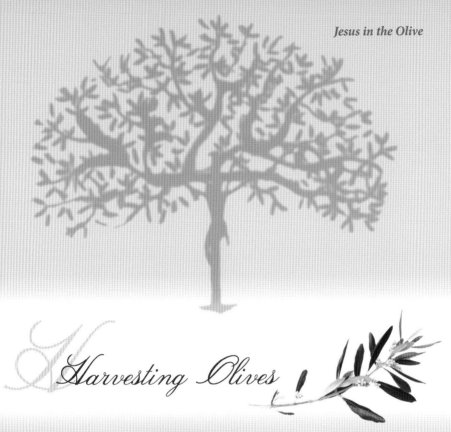

Harvesting Olives

In the Holy Land, olives were harvested in a very injurious way. They would use sticks to beat the tree, causing the olives to fall to the ground. Because of this

(003) Old twisted olive tree

harvest method, the smaller branches would be damaged and not produce any olives the following season. This could be a good reason for the tree only producing a favorable crop every other year. Why did they practice this method of harvesting? It was because their forefathers had done it this way, and the people then didn't believe in changing their customs.

As a matter of fact, Moses indicated that the same method was used by Israel when he gave the law concerning leaving some of the olive berries for the poor: "When thou beatest thine olive tree, thou shalt not go over the boughs again: it shall be for the stranger, or the fatherless, and for the widow" (Deuteronomy 24:20). Isaiah also spoke of berries left by the olive harvesters: "Yet gleaning grapes shall be left in it, as the shaking of an olive tree, two or three berries in the top of the uppermost bough, four or five in the outmost fruitful branches thereof…" (Isaiah 17:6). [1]

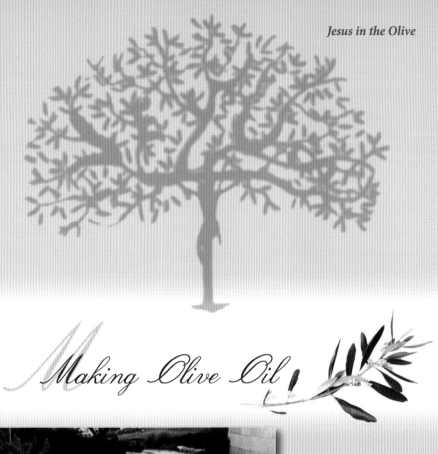

Making Olive Oil

(004)

Olive mills are used for making oil. There have been many of these instruments for the manufacture of oil located in Israel. The first press was performed by using a press that consisted of a large round bowl that had another large round wheel-like stone, with a beam through the middle like the previous picture shows. This was called the crushing stone.

This was used in the first press to crush the olives. After the olives were crushed, the fleshy part of the olive would sink to the bottom and the oil would rise to the top. This oil was the best oil (extra virgin). After the first press, what was left of the olive was put into round shaped baskets, called "mash sacks" and placed under a beam press to extract even more oil. This was the second press. At times, especially during an unfavorable crop season, this process was repeated for the third time. In Bible Times, there were two kinds of olive presses. The olive press used when Jesus was alive was a press beam. The mash sacks were placed towards the front of the beam under a round pressing board. Large stones were put towards the

(005)

end of the beam, to weigh down the beam that was resting upon the olives that were in the mash sacks. The oil would drain into collecting bowls, as you can see, to the left of the round pressing board and mash sacks. This was called the second press.

Water was mixed with the olive paste to help speed up the sinking of the flesh of the fruit. The water, olives and oil were in a container called a vat or holding box. The water and olive fluid was drained from the side of this vat. Olive oil is lighter than water, thus causing it to float toward the top. The water was then separated from the oil. The first pressing brought the best oil. The second pressing also brought good quality oil, just not as good as the first

(006)

pressing. At times, there was a third pressing to make sure that all oil was extracted from the olive paste. The Romans went through the process of pressing and separating olives and oil up to ten times. As the olives are pressed, the liquid from it has a brownish-red color to it. A few hundred years after the time of Christ, the screw press was invented (Pictures of the screw press can be seen later.).

Another Bible-time way of making oil was to tread the olive berries with the feet. This primitive method was mentioned by the prophet Micah: "...Thou shalt tread the olives, but thou shalt not anoint thee with oil..." (Micah 6:15). [1]

(007)

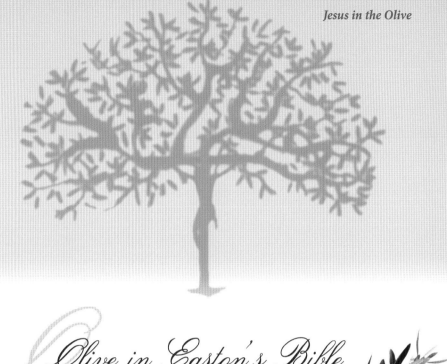

Olive in Easton's Bible Dictionary

This tree yielded oil which was highly valued. The best oil was from olives that were plucked before being fully ripe, and then beaten or squeezed (Deuteronomy 24:20; Isaiah 17:6, 24:13). It was called "beaten," or "fresh oil" (Exodus 27:20). There were also oil-presses, in which the oil was trodden out by the feet (Micah 6:15). (James 3:12) calls the fruit "olive berries."[2]

Olive in Fausset's Bible Dictionary

Its foliage is the earliest mentioned (Genesis 8:11). Tradition from Noah's days has ever made it symbolize peace. It is the emblem of "fatness" in the oldest parable (Judges 9:8-9). Emblem of the godly (Psalm 52:5; Psalm 52:8), in spirit constantly dwelling "in the house of God".... The saint's children are "like olive plants round about his table" (Psalm 128:3). The old olive sends out young suckers which spring up round the parent tree, and which in after ages, when the parent's strength fails, shelter it on every side from the blast. It is the characteristic tree of Judea on Roman coins, (Deuteronomy 8:8).... Emblem of Judah's adoption of God by grace (Jeremiah 11:16;

Romans 11:17), also of joy and prosperity. The Gentile church is the wild twig "engrafted contrary to nature" on the original Jewish olive stock; it marks supernatural virtue in the stock that it enables those wild by nature to bear good fruit; ordinarily it is only a superior scion that is grafted on an inferior.... The wood, fine grained, solid, and yellowish, was used for the cherubim, doors, and posts (1 Kings 6:23; 1 Kings 6:31-33). The tree was shaken to get the remnant left after the general gathering (by "beating," Deuteronomy 24:20), Isaiah 24:13; image of Israel's "remnant according to the election of grace." The least breeze makes the flowers fall; compare Job 15:33, "he shall cast off his flower as the olive," i.e. the least blast sweeps away in a moment the sinner's prosperity. The tree poetically is made to cast off its own blossom, to mark that the sinner brings on his own ruin (Isaiah 3:11; Jeremiah 6:19). It thrives best in a sunny position.... The trunk is knotty and gnarled, the bark smooth and ash colored. Its growth is slow, but it lives very long. The leaves are grey green, not deciduous, suggestive of tenacious strength. Used as illuminating oil in the tabernacle (Exodus 39:37; Leviticus 24:2; Zech4:12). [3]

Olive in Smith's Bible Dictionary

The olive was among the most abundant and characteristic vegetation of Judea. The olive tree grows freely almost everywhere on the shores of the Mediterranean, but it was peculiarly abundant in (Israel).... Oliveyards are a matter of course in descriptions of the country like vines and cornfields. (Judges 15:5; 1Samuel 8:14) The kings had very extensive ones. (1Chronicles 27:28) Even now (it) is very abundant in the country. Almost every village has its olive grove. Certain districts may be specified where at various times this tree (has) been very luxuriant. The cultivation of the olive tree had the closest connection with the domestic life of the Israelites (2Chronicles 2:10) their trade, (Ezekiel 27:17; Hosea 12:1) and even their Public ceremonies and religious worship. In Solomon's temple the cherubim were "of olive tree," (1Kings 6:23) as also the doors, vs. (1Kings 6:31, 32) and posts. ver. (1Kings 6:33) The wind was dreaded by the cultivator of the olive for the least ruffling of a breeze is apt to cause the flowers to fall. (Job 15:33) It is needless to add that the locust was a formidable enemy of the olive. It happened not unfrequently that hopes were disappointed, and that "the labor of the olive failed." (Habakkuk 3:17) As to the growth of the tree, it thrives best in warm and sunny situations. It is of moderate height, with knotty gnarled trunk and a smooth ash-colored bark. It grows slowly, but lives to an immense age. Its look is singularly indicative of tenacious vigor, and this is the force of what is said in Scripture of its greenness, as emblematic of strength and prosperity. The leaves, too, are not deciduous. Those who see olives for the first time are occasionally disappointed by the dusty color of their foliage; but those who are familiar with them find an inexpressible charm in the rippling changes of their slender gray-green leaves.... The olive grows from 20 to 40 feet high. In general appearance it resembles the apple tree; in leaves and sterns, the willow. The flowers are white and appear in June. The fruit is like a plum in shape and size, and at first is green, but gradually becomes purple, and even black, with a hard stony kernel, and is remarkable from the outer fleshy part being that in which much oil is lodged, and not, as is usual, in the almond of the seed. The fruit ripens from August to September. It is sometimes eaten green, but its chief value is in its oil. The wood is hard, fine beautifully veined, and is (often) used for cabinet work. [4]

Olive Oil and Olives in Bible Times

Some use is made of the pickled berry of the olive, but the bulk of the fruit is used to make oil. In the Orient, olive oil usually takes the place of butter, and is largely used in cooking meals. A survey of several scriptures will indicate how important olive oil was considered. The widow who fed Elijah said to him: "…I have not a cake, but an handful of meal in a barrel, and a little oil in a cruse…" (I Kings 17:12). She had been depending largely on bread and oil for her food, but the supply of both was about gone. The miracle of Elijah was the multiplication of that supply: "And the barrel of meal wasted not, neither did the cruse of oil fail, according to the word of the LORD, which he spake by Elijah" (I Kings 17:16). [1]

Olive oil was considered one of the great sources of wealth in the Ancient days of King Solomon (I Kings 5:11; II Chronicles 2:10). Solomon gave to Hiram each year in return for services rendered by his men, among other things, twenty thousand baths of oil, one bath being about six gallons (approximately120,000 gallons). The prophets Ezekiel and Hosea make mention of the exporting of oil to other lands (Ezekiel 27:17; Hosea 12:1).

Oil has been used for a great variety of purposes in the Orient. It largely took the place of butter in eating, and for cooking purposes, it was used in place of animal fat. And, olive oil was used almost exclusively for light in lamps. The most famous example of this is "the ten virgins, which took their lamps, and went forth to meet the bridegroom" (Matthew 25:1). Olive oil is used today, in Bible lands, in the manufacturing of soap, and it is quite likely that it was so used in Bible days. The oil was often used for anointing the body and was used many times in various religious ceremonies. It formed a part of the meal offering (Leviticus 2:1). The prophet was anointed with oil when he took over his duties (I Kings 19:16). The priest was also anointed with oil when he took over his duties (Leviticus 8:12). And, the king was anointed either by a prophet or by the priest (I Samuel 16:13; I Kings 1:34). During New Testament times, the sick were anointed for the healing of their bodies (Mark 6:13; James 5:14). Also, oil was considered a symbol of abundance (Deuteronomy 8:8), and a lack of it was a symbol of want (Joel 1:10).
[1]

The olive tree has been considered a symbol of peace ever since the dove was sent out by Noah. In fact, historically after a war, an olive branch was given to show peace between the engaging parties. Throughout the Bible, oil is often used to symbolize the

Holy Ghost.

Traveling with Food

Travelers going a distance will carry food with them, which may include bread, parched grain, dried olives, dried figs, and dates. Most travelers in the East now, as in the days of Jesus, will not go any distance from home without taking barley bread or meal or parched grain sufficient to last for one or two days. The workingman of the East usually has some olives in his bag when he leaves home for his daily work. [5]

Lessons from the Olive Tree in the Book of Psalms

Faithfulness and steadfastness are primarily what the olive tree symbolizes: "But I am like a green olive tree in the house of God: I trust in the mercy of God for ever and ever" (Psalms 52:8). As long as the olive tree is alive, it will always be green and produce olives. The olive tree will live and produce fruit in almost every type of condition (except the extreme bitter cold). It doesn't matter if it's wet or dry, hot or cold, rocky or fertile soil, on a hill or down in the valley. This verse of scripture teaches us that no matter what conditions we may be in or what we may face along life's road, we should always remain faithful to God and always produce fruit. It doesn't matter what age the olive tree is, whether it be five years old or two thousand years old, it will produce fruit. As long as it is alive, there will be olives on its branches.

"Thy wife shall be as a fruitful vine by the sides of thine house: thy children like olive plants round about thy table" (Psalms 128:3). If you ever have the opportunity to see some olive trees, you most likely will find ten or more shoots growing up around them. If these shoots are allowed to grow, they will protect and help the tree they're growing around. Even if you cut down one of these trees, the shoots around it will still continue to grow until they become mature trees themselves. So, as long as the roots are intact, the roots will produce more olive trees. God has given the commandment several times in scripture to be "fruitful and multiply." In Psalms 127:3, "Lo, children are an heritage of the Lord: and the fruit of the womb is his reward."

(008) Olive grove in Provence, France

Grafting: A Look at Our Root

The customary process of grafting was by locating a wild olive tree. The wild olive tree was cut off close to the ground, thus leaving a stump. Then branches from a cultivated tree were grafted into the stump (stock) of the wild olive tree. The part below became root and feeder for the engrafted branches.

In the book of Romans, chapter 11, Paul described the relationship between Israel and the Church through the most dramatic image of the olive tree in the Bible (It would be good for you to read this chapter.). In chapter 11, the covenants and promises to Israel are portrayed by the olive tree. We know that a tree is only growing and producing because of the root. The "Root" is the Word of God. The natural branches, which were broken off, are the people of Israel. The Gentile Christians are the "wild" branches that were grafted in among the "natural" branches, and according to Romans 11:17, "...and with them partakest of the root and fatness of the olive tree." Paul said in verse 24 that we were grafted in "contrary to nature." The way God instituted us, the Gentiles, the "wild" branches, was not by the customary process of grafting; instead, it was the very opposite, contrary to nature. Anyone, who has any knowledge of grafting olive trees, knows that you cannot graft a wild olive tree into a tamed tree and have it become a "good" fruit bearing tree. But, regardless of that fact, that's the way God did it. You see, His thoughts are above our thoughts, and His ways always seem to be contrary to what we think. Romans11:18-21 says, "Boast not against the branches. But if thou boast, thou bearest not the root, but the root thee. Thou wilt say then, The branches were broken off, that I might be grafted in. Well; because of unbelief they were broken off, and thou standest by faith. Be not highminded, but fear: For if God spared not the natural branches, take heed lest he also spare not thee." Since the branches only remain by faith, we have no right to boast, but rather, to fear and be thankful for God's grace and mercy towards us. Romans 11:28 states, "As concerning the gospel, they are enemies for your sakes: but as touching the election, they are beloved for the father's sakes." This lets us know that we should not have any hatred, or become the enemy of the "branches" who were broken off, but that we should have love and mercy towards them. If it weren't for them, we wouldn't have been made partakers of the "Root."

You see, there is only one tree, and we the wild branches have been granted the right to a new life from the already established tree. If we are not grafted into Christ, who is the "Living Root," and do not become fruit bearing branches, we are but "wild and useless olive trees." Matthew 7:19-20 explains, "Every tree that bringeth not forth good fruit is hewn down, and cast into the fire. Wherefore by their fruits ye shall know them." Our fruit production tells whether we are grafted into the word of God or not.

The roots and trunk of Christianity are Jewish: we are but branches grafted on a mighty, living tree which God has tended lovingly for two thousand years. However, there will come a time when the Gentile door will be shut; after that, the natural branches shall return unto the Tree. Romans 11:25 explains, "For I would not, brethren, that ye should be ignorant of this mystery, lest ye should be wise in your own conceits; that blindness in part is happened to Israel, until the fulness of the Gentiles be come in." When the Jews are restored, they will not enter into a new church, but, according to verse 24, shall be grafted into their own olive tree: "For if thou wert cut out of the olive tree which is wild by nature, and wert grafted contrary to nature into a good olive tree: how much more shall these, which be the natural branches, be grafted into their own olive tree?"

We didn't become a new tree, but rather an extension to God's plan.

We can clearly see that God had purposed an extension to His plan, for the Gentiles, as far back as Abraham. God had promised Abraham that he would be the father of a multitude of nations. In Genesis17:4, "As for me, behold, my covenant is with thee, and thou shalt be a father of many nations." We see it again, in Joseph, who married an Egyptian woman. Ephraim, one of Joseph's two sons, was promised that through him, there would be a multitude of nations: "…but truly his younger brother shall be greater than he, and his seed shall become a multitude of nations" (Genesis 48:19). We see this thought picked up again in the woman Rahab who had been saved from the destruction of Jericho and was allowed to join the people of Israel. In Joshua 6:25, "And Joshua saved Rahab the harlot alive, and her father's household, and all that she had; and she dwelleth in Israel even unto this day; because she hid the messengers, which Joshua sent to spy out Jericho." Again, in Isaiah 11:10, "And in that day there shall be a root of Jesse, which shall stand for an ensign of the people; to it shall the Gentiles seek: and his rest shall be glorious." We see it again in the Moabite, Ruth. Not only was she allowed into Israel, but she became the great-grandmother of King David. Perhaps, through the life of Ruth, we get a visual example of what the engrafting into the olive tree, discussed in Romans 11, is all about. Then, in the book of Acts, chapter 2 verses 38-39, Peter declared, "Repent, and be baptized every one of you in the name of Jesus Christ for the remission of sins, and ye shall receive the gift of the Holy Ghost. For the promise is unto you, and to your children, and to all that are **afar off**, even as many as the Lord our God shall call." In chapter 10 of the same book, we see that the door to the Gentiles was opened, starting at the household of Cornelius: "Wherefore remember, that ye being in time past Gentiles in the flesh, who are called Uncircumcision by that which is called the Circumcision in the flesh made by hands; That at that time ye were without Christ, being aliens from the commonwealth of Israel, and strangers from the covenants of promise, having no hope, and without God in the world: But now in Christ Jesus ye who sometimes were far off are made nigh by the blood of Christ" (Ephesians 2:11-13). It is time that the Church learns to live in humility and understands what it means to be that "wild olive branch" that was graciously grafted in by God to receive the promises and hope that we now have.

(009) Grafted olive tree in Nazareth village

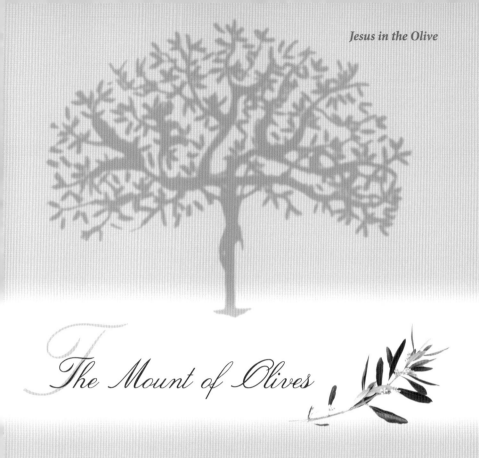

The Mount of Olives

The Mount of Olives, or Mount Olivet, received its name because of the olive groves that once covered its slopes. The Mount of Olives is one of three peaks of a mountain ridge which runs for 2.2 miles east of Old Jerusalem across the Kidron Valley and rises over 200 feet above it. The Mount of Olives was the place where several important, key events of Bible history took place. Some of the most important people of the Bible walked upon or near the Mount of Olives at some time in their lives. According to the scriptures, Jesus must have really enjoyed being here, since He visited there often, not to mention walking over it.

Here's what the scriptures say concerning the Mount of Olives:

-In the Old Testament:

The first mention of the Mount of Olives is when King David fled to escape the rebellion of Absalom. 2 Samuel 15:30 says, "And David went up by the ascent of mount Olivet, and wept as he went up, and had his head covered, and he went barefoot: and all the people that was with him covered every man his head, and they went up, weeping as they went up."

King Solomon, after he became corrupt, built pagan "high places" there. "Then did Solomon build an high place for Chemosh, the abomination of Moab, in the hill that is before Jerusalem, and for Molech, the abomination of the children of Ammon. And likewise did he for all his strange wives, which burnt incense and sacrificed unto their gods" (1 Kings 11:7-8). The mount, which later became known as the "Hill of Corruption", was infamous for idol worship up until the king of Judah, King Josiah, destroyed all the idolatrous altars. 2 Kings 23:13-14 reported, "And the high places that were before Jerusalem, which were on the right hand of the mount of corruption, which Solomon the king of Israel had builded for Ashtoreth the abomination of the Zidonians, and for Chemosh the abomination of the Moabites, and for Milcom the abomination of the children of Ammon, did the king defile. And he brake in pieces the images, and cut down the groves, and filled their places with the bones of men."

It was here that Ezekiel had the vision of the cherubims and the glory of the God (Ezekiel 11:22-23): "Then did the cherubims lift up their wings, and the wheels beside them; and the glory of the God of Israel was over them above. And the glory of the Lord went up from the midst of the city, and stood upon the mountain which is on the east side of the city."

It was from here that the people, after hearing the word of the Lord from Ezra and commandment from Nehemiah, gathered olive branches for the first Feast of Tabernacles since their return from the exile of Babylon: "And that they should publish and proclaim in all their cities, and in Jerusalem, saying, Go forth unto the mount, and fetch olive branches, and pine branches, and myrtle branches, and palm branches, and branches of thick trees, to make booths, as it is written" (Nehemiah 8:15).

-In the New Testament:

As previously stated, Jesus regularly went up onto the Mount of Olives (Luke 22:39): "And he came out, and went, as he was wont, to the mount of Olives; and his disciples also followed him." We also learned from the scriptures that He had friends in Bethany, namely Lazarus and his sisters, Mary and Martha. In order to reach Bethany, one must walk over the Mount of Olives to get there. So, every time Jesus went there to visit, He traveled over it. In Matthew 24:1-51, Jesus gave the Olivet prophecy which is named after the mount. When Jesus made His triumphal entry on a donkey and her colt into Jerusalem, this took place over and down the Mount of Olives as can be read in Luke 19:28-44. Jesus normally went there for rest, as in Luke 21:37: "And in the day time he was teaching in the temple; and at night he went out, and abode in the mount that is called the mount of Olives." Immediately after Jesus had held the Passover with his disciples, He went there, and while there, He prayed and was arrested (Luke 22:39-46). Jesus appeared to the disciples there after His resurrection, and it was from there that He ascended into heaven (Acts 1:1-12).

-In the future

Not only did Jesus ascend from the Mount of Olives, it is where He will come back. "And then shall appear the sign of the Son of man in heaven: and then shall all the tribes of the earth mourn, and they shall see the Son of man coming in the clouds of heaven with power and great glory. And he shall send his angels with a great sound of a trumpet, and they shall gather together his elect from the four winds, from one end of heaven to the other" (Matthew 24:30-31). "And his feet shall stand in that day upon the Mount of Olives, which is before Jerusalem on the east" (Zechariah 14:4).

(010) *The Mount of Olives as it is today*

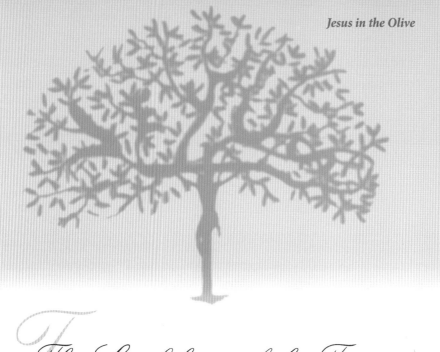

The Symbolisms of the Tree, the Olive & the Oil

The Tree

• As the olive tree is set apart from all other trees, so we, God's children, are to be set apart from all other people. Set apart is the definition of sanctification. "Sanctify yourselves therefore, and be ye holy: for I am the Lord your God" (Leviticus 20:7). The olive tree, as stated earlier, is strong, it perseveres, is steadfast and always produces fruit. "Finally, my brethren, be strong in the Lord, and in the power of his might" (Ephesians 6:10). "Therefore, my beloved brethren, be ye stedfast, unmoveable, always abounding in the work of the Lord, forasmuch as ye know that your labour is not in vain in the Lord" (1 Corinthians 15:58).

• As the olive leaf (tree) didn't pass away, this reminds us that Jesus said, "Heaven and earth shall pass away: but my words shall not pass away" (Mark 13:31).

• The tree thrives in great heat. As history has proven, the Church has always thrived during the toughest pressure and persecution. As the heat is intensified, the Church has always surpassed the advances of its opposition. Jesus did not say we wouldn't face challenges, but He did say in Matt. 16:18, "And I say also unto thee, That thou art Peter, and upon this rock I will build my church; and the gates of hell shall not prevail against it."

• The olive branch is and always has been the symbol of peace. Isaiah 9:6 states that he is the "Prince of Peace."

• As previously mentioned, the olive tree matures in 12 to 14 years. Ironically, Jesus was 12 years old (Luke 2:42) when He was in the temple with the doctors, hearing them and asking questions (Luke 2:46). In Bible times, a male was considered a youth while under the age of 40, yet considered entering manhood at age12. Furthermore, we previously read that the tree reaches its peak performance starting at age thirty, which happens to be the age of Jesus when he started his Earthly ministry.

• As the olive tree doesn't seem to have an attractive outward appearance, neither did Jesus. "For he shall grow up before him as a tender plant, and as a root out of a dry ground: he hath no form nor comeliness; and when we shall see him, there is no beauty that we should desire him" (Isaiah 53:2). On the other hand, the writers of scripture talked of the olive tree's beauty and attractiveness. Though there may be some whose "outward looks" don't attract, the Lord said he would "beautify the meek with salvation" (Psalms 149:4).

(011) Young tender olive plant

• The wood of the olive tree was used mostly for building supplies, such as posts, doors, furniture and cabinetry, as well as bowls and cooking utensils. Speaking of doors, as stated earlier, the doors of the temple that Solomon had built unto the Lord were made of wood from the olive tree. There were several doors to the entire establishment, doors leading outside, doors to the chambers and courts and so forth; but, there was only one door that lead to the main part of the temple. In this particular section was the Ark of the Covenant, and of course, the ark is where the Spirit of God was. Note that there was only one door into the Holy Temple, and it was made of olive wood. There were no other doors into the Holy Temple, the place of the presence of God, except the one. How does this reference Christ? Jesus said in John 10:9, "I am the door." In order to get into the presence of God, we must go through the door, which is Jesus. There's no other way into the kingdom, except we enter through the door. There is no other option. We cannot enter through a window, nor sneak past the gate. Heaven does not have a back door. Jesus said in John 10:1, "Verily, verily, I say unto you, He that entereth not by the door into the sheepfold, but climbeth up some other way, the same is a thief and a robber." John 14:6 says, "Jesus saith unto him, I am the way, the truth, and the life: no man cometh unto the Father, but by me." Acts 4:12 declares, "Neither is there salvation in any other: for there is none other name under heaven given among men, whereby we must be saved." I wonder if Solomon or anyone of the builders knew why the door was to be made from the olive and not of some other type of wood. It's all beginning to make sense to me now.

(012) Olive tree with blossom

• "He shall shake off his unripe grape as the vine, and shall

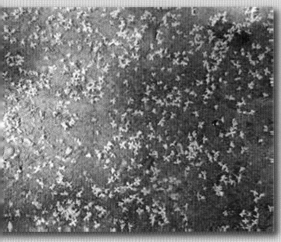

(013) Fallen olive flowers (blossoms)

cast off his flower as the olive" (Job 15:33). The tree poetically is made to cast off its own blossom, to mark that the sinner brings on his own ruin. "Then when lust hath conceived, it bringeth forth sin: and sin, when it is finished, bringeth forth death" (James 1:15).

The Olive

• The precious olive was eaten by the rich, as well as, the poor. "… and the poor have the gospel preached to them" (Matthew 11:5). "Whosoever will" can come to Jesus. It matters not your wealth, nor stature.

• Some of the worst enemies of the olive are the olive fruit fly, caterpillar, locust and extremely cold temperatures. The Church, also, has many enemies. Have you ever noticed, if you really love God and try to live a good, clean, devoted life for him, how you're looked upon? Jesus said in John 15:18-19, "If the world hate you, ye know that it hated me before it hated you. If ye were of the world, the world would love his own: but because ye are not of the world, but I have chosen you out of the world, therefore the world hateth you."

• We also read earlier from Smith's Bible Dictionary that the olive tree was singularly indicative of tenacious vigor. This means that the olive is strong, not easily pulled apart, full of energy and determination, which is the same exact characteristic of the Lord himself. "For the Lord God will help me; therefore shall I not be confounded: therefore have I set my face like a flint, and I know that I shall not be ashamed" (Isaiah 50:7). And also, Hebrews 12:2: "... who for the joy that was set before him endured the cross, despising the shame."

With that being said, we'll discuss the harvesting of the olive (which coincides perfectly with the scourging, crucifixion and resurrection of Jesus Christ, and also, the receiving of His precious gift of promise to us, the Holy Ghost, His Spirit).

• First, let's look at the flower the olive tree produces. The flower is the beginning of the olive fruit. Out of twenty flowers or blossoms, only one will be left to become an olive (Notice how even the small flower is in the shape of a cross.).

(014)

Now, we'll go to the garden scene in Gethsemane.

• The word "gethsemane" is defined as "an oil-press." It was from there, that Jesus could see all of Jerusalem. It was in the Garden of Gethsemane that the coming events suddenly overtook Jesus.

Matthew 26:39-44: "And he went a little further, and fell on his face, and prayed, (First Press) saying, O my Father, if it be possible, let this cup pass from me: nevertheless not as I will, but as thou wilt. And he cometh unto the disciples, and findeth them asleep, and saith unto Peter, What, could ye not watch with me one hour? Watch and pray, that ye enter not into temptation: the spirit indeed is willing, but the flesh is weak. He went away again the second time, (Second Press) and prayed, saying, O my Father, if this cup may not pass away from me, except I drink it, thy will be done. And he came and found them asleep again: for their eyes were heavy. And he left them, and went away again, and prayed the third time, (Third Press) saying the same words."

Part of the agony of Jesus was due to the knowledge that He was facing an unimaginable experience on the cross that involved an extremely painful and humiliating form of death. The general population believed that anyone who was crucified was cursed. In fact, the Bible states this in Galatians 3:13: "Christ hath redeemed us from the curse of the law, being made a curse for us: for it is written, Cursed is every one that hangeth on a tree."

(015)

(016) An old olive grove (The Garden of Gethsemane have looked similar to this during the time of Christ)

The most horrible "pressing upon" that Jesus' experienced, of course, was the oppressive feeling of bearing the weight of all human sin.

(018) Gethsemane today

(017) Another picture of Gethsemane as it is today

• In order to harvest the olives, sticks were used to beat the limbs or shake the tree. Remember how they hit Jesus with the reed and beat Him during the scourging? During the olive crushing process, liquid begins to emerge from the fruit. Interestingly, the liquid is brownish-red in color. The book of Luke (22: 44) reminds us that "Jesus' agony became like drops of blood falling down upon the ground," much like the drops of red liquid from the crushed fruit. Once an olive is crushed, it becomes a paste which is then smeared onto mats or burlap type fabric. Interestingly, the Hebrew word for Messiah means "to smear." The baskets or mats are stacked under a huge stone column which was called the gethsemane or oil press.

(020)

• Luke 22: 42 and 44 explain that Jesus knelt and prayed several times, saying "Father, if you are willing, take this cup from me...." Placed under pressure, more liquid is pressed out of the olive paste, much like the weight of our sins pressed out the very blood of our Savior that would result in eternal life for the world. Notice, how the olives were smashed and squeezed. This leads us to the scourging. The scourging was a beating that was used in the past to punish people, causing great trouble or suffering. The person being scourged was tied to a whipping post (which was probably, in my opinion, made of olive wood). The Centurion would order his soldiers (lictors) to scourge the prisoner to the point of "near death" using the flagrum which was designed to speedily remove flesh, even with a single lash across bare flesh. The flagrum had several strips of leather with bone, metal, glass, etc. woven into it. At this time, a great amount of blood would have flowed from the body of Jesus. He endured countless stripes to His body. This would have resembled the "reddish" color that the olives make in their first pressing. It was by these stripes that we were and are healed. Isaiah 53:2-7 says: "For he shall grow up before him as a tender plant, and as a root out of a dry ground: he hath no form nor comeliness; and when we shall see him, there is no beauty that we should desire him. He is despised and rejected of men; a man of sorrows, and acquainted with grief: and we hid as it were our faces from him; he was despised, and we esteemed him not. Surely he hath borne our griefs, and carried our sorrows: yet we did esteem him stricken, smitten of God, and afflicted. But he was wounded for our transgressions, he was bruised for our iniquities: the chastisement of our peace was upon him; and with his stripes we are healed. All we like sheep have gone astray; we have turned every one to his own way; and the Lord hath laid on him the iniquity of us all. He was oppressed, and he was afflicted, yet he opened not his mouth: he is brought as a lamb to the slaughter, and as a sheep before her shearers is dumb, so he openeth not his mouth." 1 Peter 2:24 states: "Who his own self bare our sins in his own body on the tree, that we, being dead to sins, should live unto righteousness: by whose stripes ye were healed." Scourging was, besides being crucified, the worst form of punishment. Some believe the scourging was performed before every crucifixion, and some say that it wasn't. Regardless, in Jesus' case, he suffered both. After the scourging, Pilate sought to let Him go. It was the people who decided His fate. "But they cried out, Away with him, away with him, crucify him. Pilate saith unto them, Shall I crucify your King? The chief priests answered, We have no king but Caesar" (John 19:15).

Again, in my personal opinion, I even believe the crucifix (cross) was made of olive wood. You believe the "whipping" post and the cross were made of wood from the olive tree? After doing the research of the olive tree, the olives and the oil and considering the comparisons between them and Christ, I can't help but believe the post and the cross were made from olive wood.

• So, how does the crucifixion compare to the making of olive oil? Well, remember the section pertaining to the making of olive oil? Remember how the weight was applied to the wooden beam that rested on the olives which were to be pressed? Does not this seem to be a striking image of the cross? The Bible states in Isaiah 53:4, "Surely he hath borne our griefs, and carried our sorrows." The weight of the world, with its sorrows and grief and all the sins of the people, He took to the cross and nailed it there. Some people think it was the nails that held Jesus to the cross; contrary to those beliefs, it was the Love of God that held Him there. Jesus could have come down off that cross anytime He decided to, but He stayed there just to give us eternal life. John 15:13 says, "Greater love hath no man than this, that a man lay down his life for his friends."

• Talk about being "pressed," he was pressed beyond what man can even imagine. In Psalms 22:14, "I am poured out like water, and all my bones are out of joint: my heart is like wax; it is melted in the midst of my bowels." Remember the water separation from the oil? How that the water and fluid came from the side of the vat? John 19:34 reported, "But one of the soldiers with a spear pierced his side, and forthwith came there out blood and water." Because of this, we have remission of sins. Hebrews 9:22 says, "...and without shedding of blood is no remission." Matthew 26:28 explains, "For this is my blood of the new testament, which is shed for many for the remission of sins." An added note, read Luke 24:47: "And that repentance and remission of sins should be preached in his name among all nations, beginning at Jerusalem."

The Oil

You can see now, from the things that you have read, that the oil of the olive was a precious commodity in ancient days. Following are several uses of the oil and similarities to our study.

• The oil was, and is, to be stored in a dry, cool place. In one of my readings, I read that people had once, maybe still do, put their olive oil in vats and stored them under the ground until time to be shipped. Ironically, Jesus was put in the ground (tomb) until it was time for Him to ship (resurrection).

• Olive oil was a great source of wealth during the Bible days. You read this earlier, but, here it is again. The widow who fed Elijah said to him: "I have not a cake, but an handful of meal in a barrel, and a little oil in a cruse" (I Kings 17:12). She had been depending largely on bread and oil for her food, but the supply of both was about gone. The miracle of Elijah was the multiplication of that supply, "And the barrel of meal wasted not, neither did the cruse of oil fail, according to the word of the LORD, which he spake by Elijah" (I Kings 17:16). This wasn't the only miracle concerning oil. Another miracle showed the pricelessness of the oil. II Kings 4:1-7: "Now there cried a certain woman of the wives of the sons of the prophets unto Elisha, saying, Thy servant my husband is dead; and thou knowest that thy servant did fear the Lord: and the creditor is come to take unto him my two sons to be bondmen. And Elisha said unto her, What shall I do for thee? tell me, what hast thou in the house? And she said, Thine handmaid hath not any thing in the house, save a pot of oil. Then he said, Go, borrow thee vessels abroad of all thy neighbours, even empty vessels; borrow not a few. And when thou art come in, thou shalt shut the door upon thee and upon thy sons, and shalt pour out into all those vessels, and thou shalt set aside that which is full. So she went from him, and shut the door upon her and upon her sons, who brought the vessels to her; and she poured out. And it came to pass, when the vessels were full, that she said unto her son, Bring me yet a vessel. And he said unto her, There is not a vessel more. And the oil stayed. Then she came and told the man of God. And he said, Go, sell the oil, and pay thy debt, and live thou and thy children of the rest." Like I said earlier, it was a great source of wealth.

• The oil represents the Holy Ghost, which was and still is the gift that Jesus promised us. He said in John 14:17, "Even the Spirit of truth; whom the world cannot receive, because it seeth him not, neither knoweth him: but ye know him; for he dwelleth with you, and shall be in you." Also, in Acts 1:8, "But ye shall receive power, after that the Holy Ghost is come upon you." Notice in the two previous stories, how "the oil stayed." This, too, is symbolic of another promise the Lord has given us. Matthew 28:20 states: "Teaching them to observe all things whatsoever I have commanded you: and, lo, I am with you alway, even unto the end of the world. Amen." 1 John 2:27 says, "But the anointing which ye have received of him abideth in you…."

• Having the oil was a symbol of abundance, meaning lacking nothing. David said in Psalms 23:1, "The Lord is my shepherd; I shall not want."

• The first oil derived from the olive is called "extra virgin" olive oil. The word virgin means: unsullied, chaste, fresh, unspoiled. Unsullied means: good quality, not damaged or ruined. We can obtain these same qualities if we'll only submit and yield ourselves to the Spirit of God (Oil). We have to let our selfish will, the flesh, sink to the bottom, so that the oil can rise to the top, as in separating the oil.

• The oil was used for anointing the prophet, the priest and the king before they took on the duties of the particular office. The word anoint is defined as: to smear or rub with oil or especially for consecration; to choose by or as if by divine election. Notice the first words of the definition, to smear. That was one of the definitions for Messiah. And, another definition for Messiah is the anointed one, which is also the definition of Christ. Isn't it amazing how God put all this together?

They and we anoint others with oil for the healing of our bodies, as was commanded in James 5:14: "Is any sick among you? Let him call for the elders of the church; and let them pray over him, anointing him with oil in the name of the Lord."

• The oil was also used in cooking. In fact, many people don't use butter or any other oil besides olive oil while they're cooking because of the healthful nutritional values it contains. Some even use it on salads or as a dip for bread. John 6:35 states, "And Jesus said unto them, I am the bread of life: he that cometh to me shall never hunger; and he that believeth on me shall never thirst."

• Even as most working men of the East carry olives with them on their daily business, Jesus is to be part of our everyday walk, our "daily bread."

• In times past, the oil was the main source of fuel for their lamps, which provided all the lighting they needed. This too is symbolic of Christ, for He is the light. There are many references in the Word of God that prove this. It would be good for you to take the time to search this out. There has been much written on this subject. A few of the instances include John 8:12, "Then spake Jesus again unto them, saying, I am the light of the world: he that followeth me shall not walk in darkness, but shall have the light of life." John 1:4-5 says, "In him was life; and the life was the light of men. And the light shineth in darkness; and the darkness comprehended it not." This tells us that life is in the light; but, if we don't have the oil (Spirit) in our lamps, then we are in darkness. Read the story of the Ten Virgins in Matthew 25. We must have this oil for ourselves. We can't rely on someone else's light to lead us. We are individually to let our light shine. Matthew 5:14 states, "Ye are the light of the world. A city that is set on an hill cannot be hid." Philippians 2:15 explains, "That ye may be blameless and harmless, the sons of God, without rebuke, in the midst of a crooked and perverse nation, among whom ye shine as lights in the world."

• The Romans bought, as well as produced, olive oil. They used the oil for lubricating the wheels on their chariots and carts. Lubricants are used to free up any friction or dryness, which allows for smoother movement. This is exactly how things would be if we would just apply the oil (Spirit) to our lives.

• The oil was used in cosmetics, lotions and was the base for perfumes. Psalms 149:4: "For the Lord taketh pleasure in his people: he will beautify the meek with salvation."

• The olive oil was also used as an ingredient in soap. We know what soap is used for, right? Of course we do. It's for washing and cleaning. The Bible has many references concerning this topic, also, which I think would be great for you to look into. Here are a few scriptures to help you get started. Malachi 3:2: "…for he is like a refiner's fire, and like fullers' soap." The fuller was one who fulls cloth. He would wash cloths and make them as white as snow. Psalms 51:2 states: "Wash me throughly from mine iniquity, and cleanse me from my sin." Ephesians 5:26 says: "That he might sanctify and cleanse it with the washing of water by the word." Then in Ezekiel 16:9: "Then washed I thee with water; yea, I throughly washed away thy blood from thee, and I anointed thee with oil." In 1 Corinthians 6:11, "And such were some of you: but ye are washed, but ye are sanctified, but ye are justified in the name of the Lord Jesus, and by the Spirit of our God." Acts 22:16 states, "And now why tarriest thou? arise, and be baptized, and wash away thy sins, calling on the name of the Lord."

In Revelations 7:14, "…These are they which came out of great tribulation, and have washed their robes, and made them white in the blood of the Lamb." The oil was an ingredient used in making soap. You see, the Word of God is the soap that washes and cleanses us from sin, but it's impossible for that to happen without the Holy Ghost (the oil).

Finally, I would like to conclude this study by telling of an actual experience that happened to me some ten or more years ago. I was reading, in the book of Genesis, the story of the flood. I came upon Genesis 8:11: "And the dove came in to him in the evening; and, lo, in her mouth was an olive leaf pluckt off: so Noah knew that the waters were abated from off the earth."

When I had read this verse, I said, "O live" (as in Oh Live) leaf, instead of "olive" leaf. I just backed up and re-read the verse again. As I pondered upon what I had said, and during the time of my studying for this writing, it all made perfect sense. O' LIVE!!! That's the message the dove brought back to Noah, O' Live! That's the same message God has sent to us, through Jesus Christ, O' Live! We have heard of different symbolisms and comparisons of Jesus to other things, such as a shepherd, a lamb, etc., and we know from scripture that Jesus came in the form of a servant. But, His whole being, everything He is and was, is wonderfully portrayed in the olive tree, the olive and the oil. If Jesus had not been beaten, pressed, smeared and crushed, as the olive was, then we could never have received the oil (Spirit). I pray to God, from now on when you see an olive tree, an olive or olive oil, that you will remember to thank God for … the Tree, the Olive and the Oil.

JESUS IN THE OLIVE

A factual and scriptual look at the olive and its comparison with Jesus Christ

Christopher B. Saylor

(022)

Sources:
Cover design and picture was created by the author of this book
(1) Wight, Fred H. – (Manners and Customs of Bible Lands) ch. 21 (2)
Easton's Bible Dictionary – Public Domain (3) Fausset's Bible Dictionary
- Public Domain (4) Smith's Bible Dictionary - Public Domain (5)
Wight, Fred H. – (Manners and Customs of Bible Lands) ch. 27
*All scripture is from the Holy Bible – King James Version – Public
Domain*
*Pictures:
(cover) cover picture – Jesus in the Olive – drawn by author
(001) olive tree in Assisi, Italy - flickr.com – posted by mksfly –
free to share/use commercially with modifications   (002) Gold
Roman coin dated 36 A.D. – bing.com/images – free to share images
(003) An ancient olive tree in Pelion, Greece - en.wikipedia.com –
taken by Dennis koutou – free to use image   (004, 005, 006, 019, 020)
– crusher stone & press pictures – emp.byui.edu – taken by Dr. Bruce
K. Satterfield and Bradley Ross – used by permission (007) Treading
olives – thewanderingscot.com - free to use (as posted on website
) (008) olive grove in Provence, France –free to use image - flickr.
com – taken by verseguru (009) grafted olive tree in Nazareth village
– ferrelljenkins.wordpress.com – taken by Ferrell Jenkins – permission
granted by Todd Bolen at bibleplaces.com (010)Mount of Olives –
en.wikipedia.com – file: Mount of Olives2274.jpg – free to use image
(011) young olive plant – leafsheffield.org.uk – taken by Nick Ward
– used by permission (012) olive flowers –dendroica.blogspot.com –
bing.com/images – free to share and use commercially image   (013)
Fallen olive flowers – nolanature.wordpress.com – taken by Carla
Robertson – used by permission   (014) Olive blossom – Autumn
olive - fieldbioinohio.blogspot.com – taken by Dennis Profant - used
by permission (15) prayer in the garden – bing.com/images – free
to share/use commercially – johannes-esculpiendoeltiempo.blogspot
(016) Olive trees in summer - en.wikipedia.com – taken by Art
Poskanzer - free to use image   (017) Gethsemane – apinchofsalt-
sonnleitner.blogspot.com – taken by Michael Sonnleitner – used by
permission (018) Garden of Gethsemane – en.wikipedia.com – user:
Tango7174 – free to use image (021) dove with olive leaf – bing.com/
images – public domain (022) olives on cross – drawn by author

Questions for Discussion

When you first read the title of this book, what were your thoughts?

Did you know, before reading this book, that the olive tree was such a valuable resource?

What were your thoughts when you found out that "Gethsemane" actually means "oil press"?

Did you previously know how olives were harvested or how olive oil was produced?

What are your thoughts of the "extension" God had made to His plan?

Did the "grafted" olive tree picture at the end of the Grafting chapter give you a good visual image of the message?

When you saw the picture of the Mount of Olives, did you try to imagine Jesus standing on top of it?

What were thoughts concerning the one door of the Holy Temple as compared to Jesus saying that He was the Door?

Did the picture of the olive grove bring any images or thoughts to your mind? If so, what were they?

What did you think about when reading that only one out of twenty olive flowers becomes an olive?

Put into words how you felt or thought upon seeing the "brownish-red" liquid coming from the mash sacks that were under the press. Did you think of blood?

What is your view of the author's opinion on the whipping post and the cross being made of olive wood?

Have you ever thought of the dove and Jesus bringing the same message?

Since reading this, has your view of the olive and olive oil changed? Do you think that your mind will go back to this book after seeing one of the two?

At what point in the book did you see Jesus in the Olive?

Was this, Jesus and the olive, a good comparison?

What was your overall impression of the book?

Notes:

_____

_____

_____

_____

_____

_____

_____

_____

_____

_____

Christopher B. Saylor is one who enjoys trying to find the details of stories, along with the humor in every situation. He is actively involved in all forms of children's ministries, from being a Sunday school teacher, as well as, Director of his churches VBS program. Mr. Saylor enjoys reading, studying and teaching God's Word. His passion is to inspire people to encounter the invisible God and encourage them to know and live by the word of God. He, also, loves being a husband to his wife and a father to his son. The three of them, currently live in Western Kentucky.